Becoming Without Breaking

Maintaining Me Through Every Season of Growth

Rosita Stinson

Becoming Without Breaking

Published by

Memphis, Tennessee

Scripture quotations are taken from various translations of the Holy Bible. Specific versions are not noted so as not to restrict the reader to a particular translation, as each version may carry the word needed for a reader in their current season.

About the Author

Rosita Stinson is a speaker, leadership coach, and mentor who helps women navigate career transitions and personal growth with resilience and faith. After experiencing both rapid success and unexpected setbacks, she is passionate about encouraging others to pursue sustainable success while staying true to themselves. Rosita lives in Memphis, Tennessee with her husband and family.

Dedication

To every woman who has ever risen quickly and fallen quietly.

To the one who stepped into something bigger and found herself stretched beyond comfort.

To the woman rebuilding her confidence in silence.

To the woman who walked away from what looked impressive to protect her peace.

This book is for you.

Acknowledgements

To my family, thank you for loving me through every version of myself. Through the ambition, the uncertainty, the rebuilding, and the becoming. You anchored me when I felt unsteady. Your unwavering support, your belief in me when I questioned myself, and your constant reminders of who I am, have been my grounding.

To my friends, thank you for the safe conversations, the laughter during heavy seasons, the honest reflections, and the gentle accountability. You saw strength in me before I could see it again myself.

To my Pastor, First Lady, and mentors, thank you for your wisdom, your covering, your prayers, and your guidance. You helped me interpret my experiences through growth instead of failure. You reminded me that delay is not denial and that preparation often happens in hidden places.

To every leader who stretched me-even in difficult environments, thank you. Every experience added skill, discernment, and maturity that I carry with me today.

And to the woman reading this, thank you for trusting these pages. Your becoming matters. Your journey is valid. And your growth-no matter how quiet-is significant.

With deep gratitude,
Rosita Stinson

Introduction

The Myth of Effortless Growth

We celebrate becoming.
We applaud promotions.
We post achievements.
We congratulate milestones.
We admire glow-ups.

But we rarely talk about what it <u>costs</u> to grow.

No one prepares you for the internal stretching that comes with external elevation.
No one explains how lonely growth can feel.
No one tells you that sometimes the very thing you prayed for will require a version of you that you haven't fully developed yet.

You may find yourself in a season where everything looks right on the outside.

You have responsibility.
Influence.
Access.
Opportunity.

But internally… you're tired.

Not just physically- but emotionally.

You're performing well but quietly questioning yourself.
Showing up strong but going home stretched.
Leading others while trying to lead yourself.

And at some point, you may begin to ask a question you didn't expect:
Who am I becoming in the process of all this growth?

Because growth without awareness can lead to erosion.

You can slowly abandon your boundaries.
You can silence your preferences.
You can shrink your voice to keep the peace.
You can overperform to prove your worth.
You can carry pressure so long that you forget what rest feels like.

And one day, you wake up accomplished- but unfamiliar to yourself.

This is where the conversation needs to change.

Becoming is beautiful.
But breaking is optional.

Yes, growth stretches you.
Yes, pressure matures you.
Yes, responsibility reshapes you.

But it does not have to shatter your confidence.

It does not have to rob your joy.
It does not have to erase your identity.

There is a way to evolve without losing your center.
There is a way to climb without collapsing.
There is a way to *become- without breaking*.

This book is about that way.

Table of Contents

PART I: The Pressure of Becoming

Chapter 1: The Cost of Growth

Isaiah 43:19
"Behold, I will do a new thing; now it shall spring forth…"

Growth is expensive.

And I am not just speaking financially- though sometimes it is that too.

Emotionally. Mentally. Spiritually.

Growth will require a version of you that you haven't met yet.

When I first began advancing professionally, I thought growth was about skill. Education. Opportunity. Networking.

And while those things matter, what no one told me was this:

Growth demands internal renovation.

The higher the responsibility, the deeper the self-awareness required.

You can't lead well if you don't know yourself well.

In one season, I found myself navigating new levels of responsibility. The expectations were higher. The visibility was greater. The margin for error felt smaller.

And suddenly, everything felt magnified.

My decisions. My tone. My presence. My mistakes.

I realized quickly that elevation doesn't just increase opportunity- it increases exposure.

And exposure can be intimidating if your identity is fragile.

I had to confront parts of myself I hadn't paid attention to before.

My need for approval. My discomfort with confrontation. My tendency to over-explain. My habit of carrying things alone.

Growth pulled those traits to the surface.

Not to shame me. But to strengthen me.

Because here is the truth:

If you do not grow internally at the same pace, you grow externally, pressure will reveal the cracks.

I remember nights replaying conversations in my mind. Wondering if I handled something correctly. Questioning whether I was equipped. Comparing myself to others who seemed more confident, more vocal, more certain.

Comparison is a quiet thief during seasons of growth.

It whispers:
"They're more prepared."
"They're more qualified."
"They belong here more than you do."

But growth is not about becoming someone else.

It is about becoming more fully yourself……And that requires courage.

Courage to admit what you don't know.
Courage to ask for help.
Courage to rest.

Courage to say no.
Courage to evolve your thinking.

There were moments when the stretching felt uncomfortable. Moments when I considered shrinking back to something easier. Less visible. Less demanding. Less pressurized.

But shrinking would have cost me more than stretching.

Because when you shrink to avoid pressure, you also shrink your potential.

The key is not avoiding growth. The key is growing intentionally.

Pay attention to yourself as you elevate.

Ask:
Am I changing in healthy ways?
Am I abandoning parts of myself to fit expectations?
Am I overextending to prove something?
Am I resting enough to sustain this pace?

Growth should mature you-not harden you.

It should expand your capacity-not exhaust your soul.

It should build resilience-not resentment.

I had to learn that strength does not mean silence.
Confidence does not mean perfection.
Leadership does not mean invulnerability.

And perhaps most importantly:

You do not have to break in order to become. This blessed me tremendously. So let me repeat this for you, "Sis, you do not have to break, in order to become."

Stretching is not the same as shattering.

Pressure is not the same as destruction.
And elevation is not meant to erase you.

You can grow and stay grounded.
You can advance and remain authentic.
You can evolve and still recognize yourself in the mirror.

That is the real success.

Becoming Without Breaking Reflection

Ask Yourself:

Where is growth stretching me right now?
What internal habits need to mature as my responsibilities increase?
Am I expanding - or am I overextending?

Affirmation:
"I am growing in capacity without losing my center."

Action Step:
Write down three qualities that define you beyond your professional role. Protect those qualities intentionally this week.

Scripture Reflection:
God does not introduce "new" without intention. The tension you feel is often the stretching required for expansion. Becoming is uncomfortable, but it is evidence that God is still shaping you.
Isaiah 43:19

KEY TAKEAWAYS

- *Growth requires internal development-not just external opportunity*
- *Elevation increases exposure, not just access*
- *Self-awareness is necessary for sustainable leadership*
- *Comparison will distract you from your own becoming*
- *You can stretch without losing yourself*

Chapter 2: When the Title Becomes Your Identity

2 Corinthians 4:8-9
"We are troubled on every side, yet not distressed…"

There is a subtle danger in achievement.

It doesn't announce itself loudly. It doesn't feel toxic at first. It often feels like pride.

But slowly, almost invisibly-your title can begin to replace your identity.

It starts innocently.

You work hard. You grow. You advance.

People recognize you by your position.

You introduce yourself and lead with what you do.

And somewhere along the way, you stop asking who you are without it.

I remember a season when my role carried weight. Responsibility. Influence. People relied on me. My decisions mattered. My voice carried authority.

And I was grateful for it.

But I also noticed something uncomfortable.

My mood was attached to my performance.

If I had a productive week, I felt valuable.
If I made a mistake, I felt diminished.

If someone questioned my decision, I felt personally attacked. It wasn't just feedback. It felt like a threat.

And that's when I realized something critical:

I had allowed what I did to define who I was.

Titles are powerful.

They open doors. They create access. They signal competence.

But they are temporary.

And if your confidence is built on something temporary, it will always feel unstable.

One unexpected shift. One restructure. One missed opportunity. One season of silence.

And suddenly you don't know who you are anymore.

I've watched people unravel when a title changed.
Not because they lacked ability.
But because they lacked identity outside the role.

And I had to ask myself:

If this position disappeared tomorrow-who would I be?

Would I still feel confident?
Would I still feel valuable?
Would I still feel called?
Would I still feel secure?

Or would I feel erased?

That question was uncomfortable.

Because the truth was-I wasn't completely sure.

Growth brings visibility.
But visibility also brings attachment.

You become known for something.
You become dependent upon for something.
You become respected because of something.

And it feels good.

Until it becomes the only thing.

I had to learn how to separate assignments from identity.

My role was an assignment.

My identity was deeper.

Assignments change.
Identity anchors you.

Assignments elevate you.
Identity stabilizes you.

Assignments stretch you.
Identity sustains you.

If you confuse the two, you will always feel like you're on shaky ground.

There were moments when I felt the pressure to perform perfectly- because I believed that my worth was attached to how well I carried the title.

But perfection is exhausting.

And it is impossible.

When your identity is secure, you can receive feedback without collapsing.
You can experience transition without panicking.
You can release a season without feeling erased.

Because you know this truth:

I am more than my role. I am more than my salary. I am more than my business card. I am more than what people call me in a meeting.

Titles describe what you do.
They **do not** define who you are.

And if you want to become without breaking, you must learn how to carry titles lightly.

Grateful-but not dependent.
Committed-but not consumed.
Dedicated-but not defined.

Because when the title changes and eventually it will-you must still be intact.

That is maturity. That is freedom. That is wholeness in motion.

Becoming Without Breaking Reflection

Ask Yourself:
Who am I beyond what I do?
If my role changed tomorrow, would I still feel secure?
Where have I attached my worth to performance?

Affirmation:
"My identity is anchored in who I am, not what I do."

Action Step:
List five qualities about yourself that existed before your current role- and will exist long after it.

Scripture Reflection:
Pressure is not proof of abandonment. It is often proof of assignment. You may feel pressed, but you are not crushed- and that distinction matters.
2 Corinthians 4:8-9

KEY TAKEAWAYS

- *Titles are temporary-identity must be permanent*
- *When your worth is tied to performance, instability follows*
- *Assignments change, but identity should remain anchored*
- *You must separate who you are from what you do*
- *Confidence should be internal-not dependent on position*

Chapter 3 The Silent Strain (Anchor Story)

Proverbs 4:23
"Keep thy heart with all diligence…"

There was a season when everyone around me believed I was thriving.

From the outside, I looked composed.
Capable.
Confident.
In control.

I was managing responsibilities. Solving problems. Leading conversations. Producing results.

And I was tired.

It wasn't the type of tiredness that sleep fixes.

It was the kind that builds quietly when you are the strong one for everyone else.

I became the dependable one.

The one who could handle it. The one who didn't complain. The one who would "figure it out."

And I did and did a darn good job at it too.

But what no one saw was the late nights when I questioned whether I could sustain that pace.

The internal conversations where I asked myself:
"Why does this feel heavier than it looks?"
"Why do I feel alone in this?"
"Why am I carrying this silently?"

The truth was, I had mastered competence- but neglected vulnerability.

I didn't want to seem incapable. I didn't want to appear overwhelmed. I didn't want to disrupt the image of strength people had of me.

So, I absorbed the pressure.

And pressure absorbed in silence eventually becomes strain.

The moment that shifted everything wasn't dramatic.

It was subtle.

I realized I had not asked for help in months.

Not because I didn't need it.
But because I had convinced myself that strong people shouldn't.

That realization humbled me.

Because strength is not silence. Strength is not isolation. Strength is not self-neglect.

True strength includes self-awareness.

It includes knowing when to delegate.
When to rest. When to speak. When to say, "I need support."

That season taught me that *becoming without breaking* requires honesty.

Not just with others. But with yourself.

Scripture Reflection:

Growth means nothing if you lose yourself in the process. Guarding your heart protects your calling. Becoming without breaking requires boundaries.

Proverbs 4:23

KEY TAKEAWAYS

- *Strength is not silence-it includes asking for support*
- *Carrying everything alone leads to internal strain*
- *Vulnerability is a part of true strength*
- *Self-awareness reveals when you are overextending*
- *You are not meant to carry every weight by yourself*

PART II: The Stretch and the Fall

Chapter 4: When the Rise Is Too Fast

Genesis 12:1
"Get thee out of thy country…unto a land that I will shew thee."

There was a season when opportunity came quickly.

Too quickly.

I had built a strong foundation in an established industry. I understood the rhythm of it. The expectations. The culture. I had stability. I had reputation. I had experience that felt secure.

And then a higher role presented itself.

More visibility. More authority. More influence. More advancement.

On paper, it looked like growth.

And in many ways, it was.

But I did not fully count the cost.

Sometimes elevation comes wrapped in excitement, and we mistake acceleration for alignment.

The rise felt validating. It felt like confirmation. It felt like proof that I was ready.

So, I stepped.

Confident. Hopeful. Ambitious.

And then everything shifted.

The environment was not what I expected.

The culture was misaligned.
The leadership dynamics were unstable.
The support I assumed would be present was absent.

The role added skills- yes.
It stretched me- absolutely.
It sharpened my discernment.
It expanded my experience.

But the overall environment?

It was HORRIFIC.

And I don't use that word lightly.

It was the kind of experience that tests your resilience daily.
The kind that makes you second-guess your instincts.
The kind that drains you quietly.
The kind that makes you question whether you misunderstood the assignment entirely.

I tried to adjust. I tried to endure. I tried to "make it work."

Because walking away from a higher title feels like failure.

And I did not want to be seen as someone who couldn't handle pressure.

But there is a difference between pressure that grows you and environments that break you. (Let this settle in your spirit)

And wisdom is knowing the difference.

Leaving that role was not impulsive.
It was prayerful. It was thoughtful. It was painful.

And it felt like stepping into uncertainty.

I left the position- but the experience did not immediately leave me.

What followed was a long season of self-doubt.

Did I move too soon?
Was I truly ready?
Did I overestimate my capacity?
Did I misread the opportunity?
Was I ever supposed to be there?

When a high position ends unexpectedly, it can feel like your competence is on trial.

Even when the environment was unhealthy.
Even when the decision was wise.
Even when walking away was necessary.

Instability followed.

I searched… I interviewed…. I waited…(Step and Repeat)

And waiting after a fall feels heavier than waiting in obscurity.

Because now you are not just waiting- you are rebuilding confidence.

There were moments when I questioned whether I was worthy of walking in rooms at that level again.

The doubt wasn't loud.

It was subtle.

A hesitation in my voice. A shrinking in my posture. A second-guessing of my resume.

A quiet wondering if I had "peaked too soon."

But what I did not realize at the time was this:

I was being built.

That season was not punishment.
It was preparation.

It was humbling. It was refining. It was recalibrating my motives.

I had stepped into a role quickly.
But I had not fully processed the internal maturity required to sustain that level long-term.

The plummet did not disqualify me.

It deepened me.

It strengthened my discernment.
It taught me to evaluate culture as seriously as compensation.
It taught me to count emotional cost-not just career advancement.
It taught me that quick elevation requires even quicker grounding.

And even in the instability……**I WAS KEPT**. (Insert praise break)

My needs were met.
Doors eventually opened.
Provision arrived.
Strength renewed itself.
Confidence rebuilt slowly-but sturdily.

I did not collapse. I did not disappear. I did not become bitter.

I became wiser.
And here is what I now know:
Not every fast rise is meant to be permanent.
Not every high title is meant to be sustained immediately.
Not every opportunity is aligned just because it is elevated.

Sometimes we step out too soon.
Sometimes we move faster than our foundation.
Sometimes ambition outpaces alignment.

But even then- grace covers. Even then- growth happens. Even then- nothing is wasted.

You may lose a position. You may lose stability. You may lose momentum.

But you do not have to lose yourself.

What felt was a plummet, was actually a strengthening season.

It forced me to ask:

Why do I want elevation?
What kind of environment sustains me?
Who am I when the title is gone?
Is my identity stable enough to survive instability?

Those questions built something in me that success alone never could.

And now when opportunity presents itself, I move differently.

Slower. Wiser. More discerning. More anchored.

Because *becoming without breaking* sometimes means learning from the fall.

And recognizing that even in the fall- You **were kept** (I recommend a praise break here also sis!).

Becoming Without Breaking Reflection

Ask Yourself:

Have I ever stepped into something too quickly because of the title?
Did I evaluate culture and sustainability — or just compensation and position?
What did my last disappointment actually build in me?

Affirmation:
"What looked like a setback was strengthening my foundation."

Action Step:
Write down three lessons from a professional disappointment that now serves you.

Scripture Reflection:
Separation is not punishment-it is preparation. God often reduces your surroundings before He expands your territory. Loneliness can be a corridor to destiny.
Genesis 12:1

KEY TAKEAWAYS

- *Not every opportunity is aligned-some are assignments for growth*
- *Fast elevation requires deeper grounding*
- *Environment matters just as much as opportunity*
- *Walking away can be wisdom-not failure*
- *Even in missteps, nothing is wasted*

Chapter 5: When Stability Shifts

Psalm 147:3
"He heals the broken heart…"

After leaving that elevated role, I expected clarity to come quickly.

I thought once I made the courageous decision to walk away, relief would immediately follow.

Instead, what followed was instability.

Interviews that seemed promising- and then silence.
Opportunities that almost aligned- but didn't.
Conversations that felt hopeful- but never materialized.

Waiting after a fall feels different than waiting before a rise.

Before elevation, waiting feels like anticipation.

After elevation collapses, waiting feels like questioning.

I had already proven I could operate at a certain level. I had already stepped into visibility.
I had already carried responsibility.

So, when the next role didn't arrive quickly, self-doubt tried to return.

Not loudly…….But subtly.

Maybe that role was a stretch beyond me. Maybe I am not as strong as I thought.
Maybe I moved too fast. Maybe that was my peak.

Self-doubt rarely screams. It whispers.

And if you're not careful, you begin negotiating with it. Instability tests your internal narrative.

When your resume says one thing, but your current reality says another, you have to decide which voice you will believe.

I had to learn how to separate circumstance from identity.

Circumstances shift. Identity must remain steady.

That season forced me to rebuild confidence- but this time from a healthier place.

Not confidence rooted in title. Not confidence rooted in applause. Not confidence rooted in fast movement.

But confidence rooted in:

Experience. Resilience. Self-awareness. And quiet faith.

There is something powerful about surviving instability without becoming unstable internally.

My finances were managed. My needs were met. Support showed up. Doors eventually opened.

It did not happen on my timeline.

But I was **KEPT**. (Insert praise break)

And sometimes being kept is -the miracle.

I began to see that this was not a season of demotion.

It was a season of development.

A recalibration of identity. A strengthening of discernment. A purification of motive.

I was learning how to hold ambition without urgency.
Learning how to desire elevation without desperation.

Learning how to trust that what is aligned will not require self-abandonment.

That season rebuilt my confidence-not loudly, but solidly.

I no longer wanted quick rise. I wanted sustainable growth.

And that shift changed everything.

Becoming Without Breaking Reflection

Ask Yourself:
Is my confidence rooted in position or in growth?
What is instability teaching me about myself?
Where is grace sustaining me right now?

Affirmation:
"I am steady even when my circumstances are shifting."

Action Step:
Write down evidence that you are being sustained- even in uncertainty.

Scripture Reflection:
Healing is not always loud or dramatic. Sometimes it happens quietly while you keep moving forward. God restores you even as you rise.
Psalm 147:3

KEY TAKEAWAYS

- *Instability reveals where your confidence is rooted*
- *Your identity must remain steady even when circumstances change*
- *Self-doubt often whispers-it doesn't always shout*
- *Being sustained is evidence of grace, even in uncertainty*
- *Growth continues-even in waiting seasons*

Chapter 6: Counting the Cost Before You Leap

Galatians 6:9
"Let us not be weary in well doing…"

Ambition is not the enemy.

But unchecked ambition can be expensive.

There is a difference between stepping forward with discernment and leaping because something shines.

When the higher role came to me, I evaluated the surface:

Title.
Salary.
Influence.
Visibility.
Advancement.

What I did not evaluate deeply enough was:

Culture.
Leadership health.
Emotional sustainability.
Long-term alignment.
Internal readiness.

We are often taught to measure opportunity by increase.

More money. More authority. More access.

But maturity teaches you to measure by alignment.

Does this environment match my values?
Will this leadership stretch me or strain me?

Can I grow here without eroding?
Is the pace sustainable?
Is my foundation strong enough to handle this level?

Sometimes we count the financial gain but ignore the emotional cost.

Sometimes we calculate promotion but not peace.
And sometimes we leap because the rise feels validating.

After my experience, I began asking different questions before making decisions.

Not fearful questions. Wise questions.

<u>Questions like:</u>
Why do I want this?
Is this aligned with who I am becoming?
Am I chasing validation or responding to calling?
If this becomes difficult, do I have the internal maturity to endure it?
Am I prepared to lose comfort for growth?

Counting the cost is not negativity.

It is stewardship.

Stewardship of your energy. Stewardship of your mental health. Stewardship of your confidence. Stewardship of your long-term sustainability.

There is also an internal cost many people overlook.

Rapid elevation magnifies insecurity if insecurity is unresolved.

Higher visibility exposes character gaps.
Greater responsibility amplifies emotional immaturity.

Expanded influence requires deeper self-regulation.
If you rise quickly without internal anchoring, pressure will reveal what preparation did not solidify.

And that is not failure. It is feedback.

I now understand that preparation is not only about skill acquisition. It is about identity stabilization.

It is about learning to say:
"I am ready to grow, but I will not abandon myself to get there."

Before you leap, ask:

Can I sustain this pace?
Do I trust the people leading this environment?
Is this growth- or is this ego?
Will this stretch me healthily, or strain me unnecessarily?

Not every open door is aligned. Not every higher role is healthier. Not every quick opportunity is wise timing.

And here is the grace:

Even when you step too soon, you are not ruined.

You learn. You mature. You recalibrate.

But wisdom grows when reflection follows experience.

Becoming without breaking requires intentional pauses.

It requires resisting urgency. It requires grounding ambition in discernment. It requires knowing that the right opportunity will not demand self-destruction.

Now when I sense acceleration, I do not rush.

I evaluate.
I pray.
I assess culture.
I examine leadership patterns.
I consider sustainability.

And most importantly, I check my motives.

Because elevation without alignment is expensive.

And peace is too valuable to gamble impulsively.

Becoming Without Breaking Reflection

Am I attracted to this opportunity because it is aligned- or because it is impressive?
What emotional cost might this role require?
Do I feel grounded enough internally to handle this level?

Affirmation:
"I move forward with discernment, not desperation."

Action Step:
Before accepting your next opportunity, write down the visible benefits and the invisible costs.

Scripture Reflection:
Breakthrough rarely comes through bursts of passion. It comes through steady obedience. Do not confuse slow progress with stagnation.
Galatians 6:9

KEY TAKEAWAYS

- *Not every open door is meant for you*
- *Evaluate alignment-not just advancement*
- *Emotional and mental cost matters just as much as financial gain*
- *Preparation includes internal maturity-not just skill*
- *Discernment protects you from unnecessary strain*

Introducing the B.E.C.O.M.E. Framework

After my fall, my waiting, my rebuilding, I realized something important:

Experience alone does not create wisdom. Reflection does.

It wasn't enough that I had risen quickly.
It wasn't enough that I had endured instability.
It wasn't enough that I had survived doubt.

I needed language for what I learned. I needed structure for what had shaped me.

And over time, a pattern emerged.

Every lesson, every stretch, every recalibration pointed back to six anchors that now guide how I move, how I evaluate, and how I grow.

I call it the B.E.C.O.M.E. Framework.

Not because it is about achieving. But because it is about evolving with integrity.

Because listen sis, life will test every aspect of your being….

If you let it…

B- Build Before You Leap
Strengthen identity, emotional maturity, and discernment before elevation demands it.

E- Establish Identity First
Know who you are outside of any title. Roles shift. Identity anchors.

C- Count the Cost
Evaluate the invisible price- culture, leadership health, sustainability- not just compensation.

O- Observe the Culture
Skills can grow anywhere. Health cannot.

M- Maintain Boundaries
Protect energy. Protect peace. Protect long-term capacity.

E- Evolve Intentionally
Grow with grounding. Rise with wisdom. Expand without eroding.

This framework does not prevent challenges.

But it protects you from breaking under them. It allows ambition and wholeness to coexist.

And it reminds you: You are not racing toward success. You are becoming.

KEY TAKEAWAYS

- *Build before you leap-foundation matters*
- *Establish identity before stepping into new roles*
- *Count the cost beyond what is visible*
- *Observe culture before committing*
- *Maintain boundaries to preserve your capacity*
- *Evolve intentionally-not impulsively*

PART III: Rebuilding Without Hardening

Chapter 7: Reintroducing Yourself to Yourself

Hebrews 10:35-36
"Cast not away therefore your confidence…"

After instability, something unexpected happens.

You change.

Not dramatically. Not all at once. But subtly.

Your priorities shift. Your tolerance narrows. Your discernment sharpens. Your definitions of success mature.

And one day you realize:

I am not who I was before that season.

Growth changes you.

But if you move too quickly into the next opportunity, you may never pause long enough to meet the new version of yourself.

After my rebuilding season, I had to sit quietly with myself.

What do I value now?
What will I no longer tolerate?
What pace sustains me?
What kind of leadership environment allows me to thrive?
What kind of voice do I want to carry?

Before, I was ambitious. Now, I am aligned.

Before, I was eager. Now, I am discerning.

Before, I wanted to prove. Now, I want to build steadily.

Reintroducing yourself to yourself requires stillness. It requires honesty about what hurt.

Honesty about what matured. Honesty about what strengthened. It also requires releasing shame.

Tell yourself this:

- I am allowed to outgrow old mindsets.
- I am allowed to evolve beyond old ambitions.
- I am allowed to desire peace more than prestige.

Becoming without breaking means honoring the new wisdom you earned.

You are not starting over. You are starting deeper.

Becoming without Breaking Reflection

Who have I become because of my last season?
What no longer aligns with me?
What version of success feels healthier now?

Affirmation:
"I honor who I am becoming."

Action Step:
Write down three ways you have changed because of your last season. Use those insights to guide what environments and opportunities you choose next.

Scripture Reflection:
The urge to quit often appears right before growth multiplies. Endurance is not weakness-it is maturity. Stay in position.
Hebrews 10:35-36

KEY TAKEAWAYS

- *Growth changes you-pause long enough to recognize it*
- *You are allowed to outgrow old versions of yourself*
- *Reflection is necessary for aligned decision-making*
- *You are not starting over-you are starting deeper*
- *Your new standards should reflect your new awareness*

Chapter 8: Boundaries That Preserve You

Romans 12:1
"Present your bodies a living sacrifice…"

Boundaries are not walls.

They are filters.

Before my rapid rise and fall, I believed hard work solved everything.

Say yes.
Figure it out.
Stay late.
Carry the load.
Handle it quietly.

But capacity without boundaries leads to depletion.
After rebuilding, I realized something critical: If I do not define my limits, someone else will.

Boundaries protect:
Your energy.
Your time.
Your emotional stability.
Your long-term effectiveness.

Boundaries are not about rejection.
They are about preservation.

Preserving your voice.
Preserving your peace.
Preserving your health.
Preserving your identity.

Sometimes *becoming without breaking* simply means saying:

"That does not align."
"That pace is not sustainable."
"I need clarity before committing."
"I cannot carry that alone."

You can be strong and still require support.
You can be capable and still require margin.

Boundaries do not make you less committed.

They make you sustainable.

Becoming without Breaking Reflection

Where am I overextending?
What drains me unnecessarily?
What boundary would protect my peace right now?

Affirmation:
"My boundaries protect my becoming."

Action Step:
Identify one area where you are overextending and write down a boundary that would protect your energy. Commit to practicing that boundary this week.

Scripture Reflection:
True transformation begins with surrender. Becoming without breaking requires yielding, not forcing. Sacrifice strengthens what striving cannot.
Romans 12:1

KEY TAKEAWAYS

- *Boundaries protect your energy, not limit your potential*
- *Without boundaries, burnout becomes inevitable*
- *You teach people how to treat you by what you allow*
- *Saying no can be a form of self-respect*
- *Sustainability requires intentional limits*

Chapter 9: Peace Over Performance

2 Samuel 6:14
"David danced before the Lord with all his might..."

There was a time when I believed excellence required exhaustion. I believed, if I wasn't tired, I wasn't trying hard enough.

But exhaustion is not evidence of impact.

Peace is not weakness. Peace is alignment.

After instability, I no longer wanted to perform strength.

I wanted to live grounded.

Performance is fueled by pressure.
Peace is fueled by clarity.

Performance asks:
"How do I look?"

Peace asks:
"How am I internally?"

When your identity is secure, you do not need constant validation.

You can grow quietly. You can lead steadily. You can move strategically. You can say no without guilt.

Peace does not mean you lack ambition.

It means your ambition no longer controls you.

Becoming without breaking requires choosing peace repeatedly-especially when performance would impress others more.

Becoming without Breaking Reflection

Am I performing strength or living grounded?
What does peaceful success look like for me?
Where am I chasing approval?

Affirmation:
"I choose peace over performance."

Action Step:
The next time you feel pressure to prove yourself, pause and choose a response that protects your peace instead of your image.

Scripture Reflection:
Growth sometimes demands bold obedience. You cannot evolve while worrying about opinions. Freedom lives on the other side of self-consciousness.
2 Samuel 6:14

KEY TAKEAWAYS

- *Exhaustion is not proof of effectiveness*
- *Peace is a sign of alignment-not weakness*
- *Performance seeks validation-peace reflects security*
- *You do not have to prove yourself to be valuable*
- *Choosing peace protects your long-term growth*

PART IV: Becoming Whole

Chapter 10: Sustainable Success

Philippians 3:13-14
"Forgetting those things which are behind…"

Sustainable success feels different.

It is slower. It is steadier. It is less dramatic. It is more grounded.

It does not spike quickly.
It builds intentionally.

Sustainable success allows you to:

Sleep.
Laugh.
Rest.
Think clearly.
Maintain relationships.
Recognize yourself.

It is not fragile.

It does not collapse when a role shifts.
It does not evaporate when a door closes.

Because sustainable success is internal first.

It is built on:
Identity.
Discernment.
Boundaries.
Alignment.
Peace.

If the opportunity requires self-abandonment, it is not sustainable.

If the culture erodes your integrity, it is not sustainable.

If the pace destroys your health, it is not sustainable.

The goal is not just to rise. The goal is to remain whole while rising.

And that kind of success lasts.

Becoming Without Breaking Reflection

What would sustainable growth look like for me?
Am I building something I can actually sustain?
Does my success allow me to remain whole?

Affirmation:
"I pursue success that sustains me."

Action Step:
Look at one goal you are pursuing and ask if the pace allows you to remain healthy and whole. If not, identify one adjustment that would make it more sustainable.

Scripture Reflection:
Forward movement requires release. You cannot hold yesterday and reach for tomorrow. Letting go is not loss-it is alignment.
Philippians 3:13-14

KEY TAKEAWAYS

- *Success should support your life-not consume it*
- *Sustainable growth is steady, not rushed*
- *If it costs your peace, it is too expensive*
- *True success allows you to remain whole*
- *Internal stability creates external longevity*

Chapter 11: Alignment Over Acceleration

Isaiah 40:31
"They that wait upon the Lord shall renew their strength…"

There was a time when speed impressed me.

Quick promotions. Fast visibility. Rapid advancement.

Acceleration felt like proof.

Proof that I was capable. Proof that I was ready. Proof that I was seen.

But acceleration without alignment is fragile.

It moves quickly- but it does not always last.

After walking through elevation, collapse, rebuilding, and recalibration, I no longer ask, "How fast can I get there?"

I ask, "Is this aligned with who I am now?"

Alignment is quieter than acceleration.

It does not rush. It does not force. It does not demand self-abandonment.

Alignment feels steady.

It feels peaceful. It feels sustainable. It feels congruent with your values.

Acceleration often feeds ego.

Alignment feeds purpose.

Acceleration says:
"Move now or miss it."

Alignment says:
"What is meant for you will not require you to fracture."

I have learned to sit longer with decisions.
To evaluate culture carefully.
To observe leadership patterns.
To examine my own motives.

Not from fear.

But from maturity.
Because I now understand that the right opportunity will not punish me for taking time to discern.

It will still be right tomorrow.

And if it disappears because I paused to evaluate- it was not aligned to begin with.

Becoming without breaking requires choosing alignment over urgency.

It requires trusting that your timing does not have to match someone else's.

It requires believing that steady growth builds stronger foundations than fast elevation.

I do not rush anymore. I root.

I do not chase anymore. I evaluate.

I do not leap impulsively. I align intentionally.

And that shift has preserved me.

Becoming Without Breaking Reflection

Am I pursuing speed or sustainability?
Does this opportunity align with who I am becoming?
What would moving slower protect?

Affirmation:
"I choose alignment over acceleration."

Action Step:
Before your next major decision, pause and ask if the opportunity truly aligns with your values and the life you are building.

Scripture Reflection:
Waiting is not wasting. It is where hidden strength is built. Renewal often happens when no one sees.
Isaiah 40:31

KEY TAKEAWAYS

- *Speed does not equal success-alignment does*
- *What is meant for you will not require self-abandonment*
- *Waiting builds strength and clarity*
- *Discernment requires patience*
- *Moving slower can protect your future*

Chapter 12: Whole, and Still Becoming

2 Corinthians 4:16
"Though our outward man perish, yet the inward man is renewed day by day."

There is a version of success I no longer chase.

Not the loud kind.
Not the rushed kind.
Not the externally impressive kind.

Not because success is wrong…
But because I now understand wholeness.

Wholeness is not perfection.

It is integration.

It is ambition and peace coexisting.
It is strength and softness aligned.
It is growth without fragmentation.

I have risen quickly.
I have fallen unexpectedly.
I have doubted myself quietly.
I have waited longer than I wanted.
I have rebuilt more than once.

And through it all-

I was kept (insert praise break)!

Kept from bitterness.
Kept from quitting.
Kept from losing myself completely.

Becoming without breaking does not mean you never bend.

It means you do not shatter.

It means disappointment refines you but does not define you.
It means instability strengthens you but does not destabilize you internally.

It means you learn to measure success differently.

Now, success means:

Peace in my decisions.
Clarity in my motives.
Boundaries in my calendar.
Discernment in my yes.
Confidence that is not dependent on applause.

It means I can release a role without losing myself.
It means I can step into a room without performing.
It means I can wait without unraveling.
It means I recognize myself in the mirror.

And if you are in a rebuilding season right now, hear this:

Nothing was wasted.

Not the fast rise.
Not the painful exit.
Not the unstable waiting.
Not the self-doubt.

It was building depth.
It was building discernment.
It was building grounding.

You are not behind.

You are becoming.

I have seen what happens when growth outpaces grounding.

I have felt the silence after applause.

And I have learned this:

Wholeness is the real win.

You can have a title and still be fragmented.
You can have visibility and still feel invisible.
You can have responsibility and still feel insecure.

But when you are whole-

You can survive change.
You can navigate instability.
You can release roles.
You can rebuild quietly.
You can wait… without unraveling.

I no longer measure success only by position.

I measure it by:

Peace.
Alignment.
Emotional stability.
Integrity.
Sustainability.

I measure it by whether I can recognize myself
at the end of a season.

Because *becoming without breaking* means:

I stretched- but I did not shatter.
I rose- but I did not lose myself.
I fell- but I was kept.
I doubted- but I rebuilt.
I waited- but I matured.

And I am still becoming.

Not rushed.
Not frantic.
Not proving.

Just growing.

Whole.

And still becoming.

What This Journey Has Given You

As you close this book, recognize what you now carry:

You've learned how to grow without losing yourself.
You've learned how to protect your peace in pressure.
You've learned how to separate your identity from your title.
You've learned how to move with alignment instead of urgency.
You've learned that success should sustain you- not drain you.

This was never just about career.

This was about preservation.

This was about becoming… the right way.

Pause and Reflect

Take a moment and sit with this.

Not to rush.
Not to fix.
But to recognize.

Because one of the most powerful things you can do
is acknowledge where you are- without judgment.

This journey may not have looked the way you expected.
Some parts stretched you.
Some parts humbled you.
Some parts forced you to see things
you would have never chosen to confront.

But you're still here.

And that matters more than you realize.

You made it.

Not just to the end of this book…
But through every season
that tried to convince you that you wouldn't.

So, ask yourself honestly:

Where am I right now- emotionally, mentally, spiritually?
What did this season reveal about me?
What did I survive that I don't give myself enough credit for?
What am I still holding onto that I need to release?
What version of me is emerging- even if it still feels unfamiliar?

You don't need all the answers.

But it is good to recognize:

Growth is not always loud.

Sometimes it looks like quiet decisions…
like choosing peace…
like setting boundaries…
like walking away…
like starting again.

Where you are is not a failure.

It's a checkpoint.

And this version of you?

She is not behind.

She is becoming.

You may not feel fully confident yet.
You may not have all the answers.
You may still be rebuilding parts of yourself.

But don't miss this truth:

You are not who you used to be.

And that is evidence of growth.

Affirmation

"I am evolving with integrity.
I am rising with peace.
I am *becoming- without breaking.*"

A Declaration of Becoming

Read this slowly.
Let it settle.
Let it become yours.

I am not breaking-
I am becoming.

I am allowing growth to shape me
without allowing pressure to harden me.

I release the need to prove myself
through exhaustion, performance, or validation.

I give myself permission to grow
at a pace that honors my healing.

I am no longer holding onto what drained me
just because it once defined me.

I am choosing clarity over confusion.
Peace over pressure.
Purpose over appearances.

I am learning to trust myself again.

I am rebuilding-
with wisdom,
with boundaries,
and with intention.

Every experience has refined me.
Every challenge has strengthened me.
Every moment has prepared me.

I am not who I was-
and I don't need to be.

I am becoming whole.
I am becoming grounded.
I am becoming aligned.

And this time…

I am not losing myself in the process.

I am ***becoming-***
without breaking.

Final Self-Reflection

Take a moment to write your truth:

What has this season taught me about myself?

____

____

What am I releasing?

____

____

What am I becoming?

____

____

What will I protect moving forward?

____

____

Author's Note

This book <u>was not</u> written from a place of having it all together.

It was written from the middle.

From seasons where I was still trying to understand what God was doing in my life.
From moments where things looked stable on the outside… but internally, I was navigating pressure, uncertainty, and quiet battles no one else could see.

It was written while I was still trying to find my footing…
still being stretched beyond what felt comfortable…
still learning how to hold it all together.

There were moments I questioned myself more than I trusted myself.
Moments where anxiety tried to speak louder than my confidence.
Moments where I had to show up strong- while still learning how to be whole.

And yet…

Through all of it, I was kept. (YES, a praise break goes here also!!)

Kept when I wanted to walk away.
Kept when I didn't feel qualified.
Kept when I didn't fully understand the season I was in.

This book is not just about growth.

It's about what it takes to grow without breaking in the process.

It's about learning that elevation without grounding can become overwhelming.
That success without clarity can become draining.
And that becoming requires more than movement- it requires alignment.

I didn't write this as someone who has arrived.

I wrote this as someone who is still becoming.

Still learning how to trust my voice.
Still learning how to move with peace instead of pressure.
Still learning how to choose alignment over urgency.

If you find yourself in a season where things feel uncertain, stretched, or unfamiliar-
I want you to know this:

You are not behind.
You are not failing.
You are not broken.

You are becoming.

And even in the moments where it feels overwhelming…
even in the spaces where you are unsure of yourself…

You are still being shaped with intention.

Nothing you have experienced is wasted.

Not the pressure.
Not the doubt.
Not the waiting.
Not the rebuilding.

It is all working together to develop a version of you
that is not just successful-

But whole.

So, give yourself grace.
Give yourself time.
And allow yourself to grow in a way
that does not cost you your peace.

You don't have to rush this process.
You don't have to prove anything.

Just keep ***becoming***.

Without breaking.

www.ingramcontent.com/pod-product-compliance
Lightning Source LLC
LaVergne TN
LVHW020514100826
845148LV00003B/773

* 9 7 9 8 2 3 4 0 3 0 3 1 3 *